BREAKING CAMP

Also by this author:
Dream Farmer

Breaking Camp

Poems and Photographs

by

Jill Witherspoon Boyer

Detroit
LOTUS PRESS
1984

International Standard Book Number: 0-916418-52-9
Library of Congress Catalog Number: 83-82772

First Edition

Second Printing (May, 1985)

Lotus Press, Inc.
Post Office Box 21607
Detroit, Michigan 48221
(313) 861-1280

For Naomi Long Madgett
and
Julian F. Witherspoon,
my parents,
and for my Malaika.

Contents

Photographs by the author appear on the front cover and pages 21, 24, 26, 29, 35, 36, 41, and 48.

BREAKING CAMP

I.

Disengaging

Reconciliation

We are only
cell against cell
in this bed we enter from different sides
even with the passionate promise
to try one more time
this road we know so well.

In the morning I will be off to the sea
and you to your mountain.
Only the kitchen table where we brood together
will bind us to our vow.

And I will wonder
and you will not:
How many dark eons
have we traveled from each other
dead with speed?

(Do you hear me?)

To My Husband
on the Arrival of Our Daughter

Mingling waters smooth
the rocks of separateness —
    blend into song.
Then a voice no louder
    than a baby's breath
calls out in our high tide,
    "This is your place."
And the welcome overflow settles
    content upon our faces
as we listen and sing
    beneath love's shading trees.

Contest

I am water
against the hard
hard rock of you.
I know your dangerous edges
from all angles
wedged as you are
in vulnerable veins.

But I keep the way of water
always returning always
with the thought
that I may yet
leave my mark on you.

Disengagement

Let us leave
the rusted crusted crumbled
hull of us
to rot where it is.

Let the memory of unlove's hell
and its steaming
streaming foul fumes
remain with us always
so that should we ever
run across this shit again
we'll know exactly
what it is.

Disengagement #2

There is still something
I would do
if I could do something.
Or say or give.
But I don't know who you are
with your back to me
all tight and with the softness
gone.

So I make the best good-bye I can:
I will not lie to you
who I once laid my dreams on.
I won't lie and say
I don't feel something still,
like caring,
somewhere.

Wailing Times

There are those wailing times
when we petition
not for mother nor for child
but for ourselves —
that our long battles
may be finally
blessed with peace,
and that we may be comforted
when the whole universe
is clanging at our heads.

Finished

The house is down.
This and that are scattered
here and there.
From our new places, in our own time,
we each return
to stand again
where the house used to be.
And we try to make sense of it,
poking around
in the precious ash.

II.

Wearing Gypsy Bangles That Catch the Sun

Breaking Camp

Leave the things that served
          for yesterday
that serve no more.
Ashes cannot fight the dark.
Do not linger long nor settle
          in a parched corner
when there are flowers calling
          everywhere.
Sometimes it is better that we
gather up and go
wearing only gypsy bangles
that catch the sun.

Sun Song

Gnarled and quartered joy
slumps tearful into my pillow.
I have died
where faith and vagrant spirits
leave dreams unattended.
My sister, I have seen you
prostrate too.
And because I am hushed
by my sometimes gasping dreams
I hear when your Sun Song is sobbed at midnight.
But in our trudging back together
to a birth place
you and I have laced lyrics to a common song,
even when we thought the other's voice
was only distant, echoed chords.
And yes I do believe in our rising,
past ghosts with broken wings,
beyond, to heart-pitched comets.
I believe in our rising.

Houses

People pushing boxes
grieve the hollowed house
that counts its age
by the movings —
people moving up and better,
or down, till better comes.
Houses live:

The front porch swing creaks
with childhood musings
till dreams and legs have stretched beyond
the memory of Mother's nightly kneeling,
family secrets in the attic,
and the man-to-mans held on the back steps
when Daddy would press a quarter in a smaller hand
and wink.

Leaving home previews the other moves,
and questions follow answers
out of my long-ago house
where three small trees
breathed pine into the windows.

Upholding

You daily spring to life
before I have completely wrung my nightmares
from my sleep.
I rise slowly to new burdens
that I'm made grateful for
when a silly something
sends you giggling to the floor.
I uphold the laughter.
And your wiggling warmth tells me
we're going to be alright —
with a Daddy
or without.

Home-girl

(For Aleatha)

It's not like I haven't left before
you know.
Me and my fitful ways have left you
stranded for meaning
more than once
while I careened through mirages
of unresolved girl-hood
straining to become myself.
Remember when I leaped off to Brazil?

I have circled around circles —
not like you who were always certain
and straight to the point.
Our magic was different.
Still, didn't we braid it
into a comfortable caring?
And haven't we shared a sturdy place
where doors swing both ways?

But now a space and time
wider than we've known
comes and threatens me with tears.
I will try to get through the coming miles
of missing you.
While I still can, I hold you near
to finally fasten our easy closeness
and sister-ways
which will I know withstand
the distant touch.

III.

Red Soil of My Soul

Poet

You who believe in spirit things
know the hunger that drives the Muse
from cupboard to cupboard.
So prepare and offer your food:
I wish you the bounty of Africa,
and a steady hand.

Terra

Your mountains preside over glorious green,
and over me, Brazil.
Red soil of my soul,
you are the sweetest mango,
summer moonrise over Guanabara Bay —
my Carnival.

But I hear the ancient spirits
of Africa and Amazon
drumming to your bright new capital
that is squatting in the wilderness.
And they cry, "Water, water,"
for the drought-death in the North.
"We are not citizens of Samba only.
Give our people bread and books.
Give our people bread and books."

Pelourinho

Bahia, Brazil

Oh! Yansan, goddess of the Niger River,
transported to Brazil, we bid you visit upon
us your blessings and your power. Epa Rei! Epa Rei!

The faces here are mostly browns
that recall the African, the Indian, the Portuguese.
In these former slave quarters, time is measured
in hundreds of years.
The money-makers long ago
left this one-time capital of Brazil,
and the city now lies wasting
like some fallen Jaca fruit.
Only the Catholic and Yoruba saints
have remained steadfast.

In the mornings there is the smell of urine,
and yesterday's garbage.
Later, these ancient cobblestones glisten over
with the slow drizzle of a cleansing rain.
A midday meal begins to simmer in the heavy summer air
(codfish in palm oil and coconut milk, today).
From their peeling, pastel doorways
several men drift into the narrow street,
and set up a rematch of last night's checker game.

Continued on the next page

An old black woman secures her load
past the barefoot boys, who play a frantic soccer
with a stray tin-can.
She will hurry to Vasco De Gama Street,
where there is Condomblé tonight.
She will beat the Atabaque drums
and call the spirits to descend, singing,
"Epa Rei! Epa Rei!"

> *Yansan, warrior-woman, ruler of*
> *thunderbolts and fire, touch me!*
> *Epa Rei! Epa Rei!*

IV.

"You are mine in ways that matter
and I am yours."

Waiting

(For Linda and Norman)

Your light has been affirmed
            with light.
It moves about you
then within
gathering membrane, muscle
            and blood.
Your precious love-lit something
presses solidly against the heart
and waiting its turn to be
is wise already.

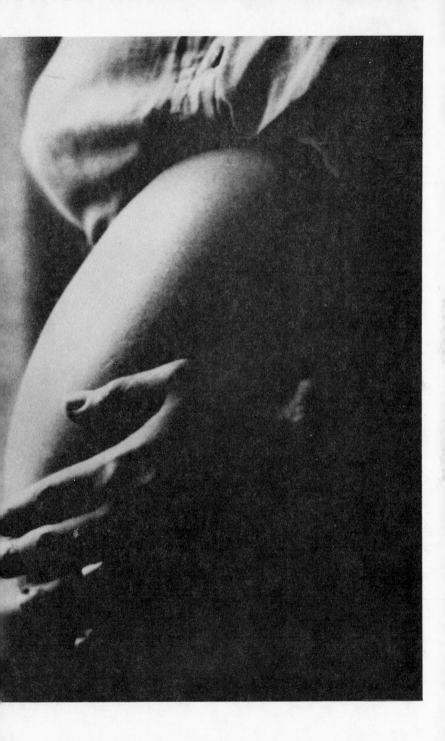

Grand

What do you remember at ninety
when what you long-ago hoped for
has either happened or won't
and you have ceased to desire
that which will not come?

What stays with you now
through all the years
that is less immediate than cataracts
and aching knees
but is real and precious to you?

Within your treasury of remembrances
keep me, old woman —
I, who was your first "grand" —
the skinny one who used to stare
up at your wide aproned hips
as you made magic
with green beans and biscuits.
And I marveled at how you stood
so eloquently beside your man,
my grandpa who always came
to dinner the first time
you called him.

Keep me
along with the son
shot down over Germany
in the war,
the family cat,
St. Louis and the friends left behind,
and the missionary society
of Bethesda Baptist Church.

Though at ninety your day seems as long
as a week
and concentration eludes
your weakening grasp,
though your thoughts flicker
like the fireflies
around your house in summers past,
remember me, old woman,
your first "grand" —
the skinny one.

Meeting Place
(For Al and Irene)

My little girl years
of gazing up
now look you straight in the eyes
when routine allows
this rare, coffee-cozy visit
between two generations.
What we embrace in each other
is the permanent weight
our lives have gathered
even when we say,
"You haven't changed a bit."
Our talk glides over time,
and flashes of who we were
haunt history's retelling
of what is now embellishment.
Still, we are richer for remembering.

Then you say your eyes are failing,
you are going blind.
And the particular present rises
and tries to lock us
into our aging, fickle bodies.
But, then and when separate nothing real
and sipping coffee,
I know I love you beyond conditions of time.

Paulette

In the third year
away
from your brownish,
high-tossed wit
I remember more details of feeling
than face —
your hand-made furniture
and home-made boys.
And it was your accessible warmth
like tasty pies steaming
in an open window
that drew me close.
In my mind I come upon you
still,
now with smiles
I keep to myself.

If I Could Tell You

(For Shari)

Thirteen
signals the emerging of fluttering sighs —
and breasts.
Somewhere you will begin to leave behind
your mother's child,
like unwanted baby-fat.
But there will be times you grieve
to call your childhood back, too.

You will paint your face a million ways
before it looks like who
you think you are today.
And you will try on other names:
Perhaps you will be "Tanya"
who needs a lighted stage
for her perfect song.
Or "Angela" who wears
heavy, purple velvet dresses
to match her melancholy of
not being understood.
But after teary, prayerful deals with God
you will awaken to be only
exactly as you are.

But a time is coming
when you will control
the magic of your stretching and growing —
though it may still cause you pain.
Your blooming will be expected and welcome
though you will always have to work at it.
You will become the greatest gift
you give yourself,
no matter what riches
the world may flash.
And while this will not be
everything you have dreamed of,
it will be enough.

Mine

How will I tell you?
What will I say
when you ask
if I carried you in my belly?
And did my back sway with the mighty
miracle of you?
What will I say when you ask
which of my dreams was awakened
by your thrashing?
And wasn't the feel of you
growing under my heart
the best dream of all?
What will I say when you ask
if I carried you?
How will I say I did not?

There is no blood between us,
this is true.
But you are mine in other ways
that count.
And I am yours.
Out of the tender growing times
my breast has learned to rise and fall
according to your breathing.
Step by baby step you came clinging
to the long embrace
that now forever binds us.
I have hovered over your dreams
with the name that I gave you,
when mine was the only name
you could say.
And I have known sleep
deep with the aura and harmony
of our days' loving.

So in your necessary questing,
when you trace the path back
to who you are
know what my heart knows —
you are mine in ways that matter.
And I am yours.

"Jelly Bean"
(For Malaika)

I fumble with the photos of the girl
they say I was.
There are times though
I recognize myself best through you.
When you are all sassy
and full of *no's*
or quietly fragile.
But, not being me, you are good beyond
       my patience,
twirling girl.
Though I motherly try to save
       your knees,
you always have your own ideas.
When I teach from an old book,
you emerge my precious broken rule.
But I am learning that we are
       women
at different times of growing,
coming and going together
into the sun of our house
each of us still becoming,
each
with our own stars to see.

Friend-friends

Friend-friends.
All-around-through-thick-and-thin
friends.
Growing-up-and-getting-down friends.
We're can't-stay-mad-too-long friends.
You and me.

We're dreaming, scheming,
hold-my-hand-I-hurt friends,
my-children-call-you-Auntie friends.
We're words-can't-even-say-it friends.
You and me.

V.

Deliberate Fires

Hex

African nose and lips
peeking from underneath
baby blankets
still light disappointment
and shame's old fires
in some black mother.
And the hex
she tucks in with this new one
is her craving to be
other than what she naturally is.
Conferring secretly with past auctioneers
she inspects baby's hair and color
to see if they are worthy
of her tenderness.
Even when she holds his need
against her breast
her look wanders and she sighs
at fairer baby faces
who buy the world's open arms
with being cute.
But after all, he is hers
and she must help him
overcome his looks
when others throw their stones
beside her own
onto his life's walkways.

George Jackson

The newsboy hands us
his death
and smiling leaves us wondering
what to do with it.
We shift from foot to foot
old discontents,
as the careful comfort in our lives
flicks off the bullet
that found the soft spot
in his back.
Still, some vague thing
about freedom
makes us nervous to know
where he went.

He falls hard into our memory
of others gone
for something or nothing.
Righteous rebel, he was tracked to the heights
of his road
that bent dangerously proud.
Though his spirit rose through deliberate fires,
he couldn't escape the ones
who sent the bullet.
But even those who knew their jobs
so well
only got his flesh,
because they couldn't strike
the awakened worth of him.

Continued on the next page

And we, reading his blood,
we jerk on tenterhooks
for fear a trail of broken chains
may lead to us.
Servants of safety, we live in our skins.
Our chorus is, "He can afford to be free,
who has nothing to lose.
But those who have jewels
must stay in the grace of thieves."
And so we pull a cover
over our weapon of will
and yield to forgetfulness of him
with already drying tears.

VI.

Settling on Peaceful Slopes

Again

If it happens at a crossing wide enough
and if the furious dust of dead ends
settles finally on peaceful slopes,
then perhaps there will be air clear enough
to restore a view that calls us to be
hopeful as a bride,
with nothing in our eyes again
but light.

Friends

The moon scatters
    on the water,
and glimmers like a million separate
    lights
we know are one.
Just as you and I,
although distinguished by apparent forms,
nonetheless emerge from kindred corners
    of the universe
and are united like a single
common thought.

No Need to Test

No need to test our touching,
only to retreat, translate and perhaps decide
this passing winter warmth of hand on hand
should not be lost to distance or to time.
Too briefly is the sun
angled on your face,
and only memory will be left
to guard the gifts
we each leave with the other.
So, let us grandly take our moment.
For what is really ours to keep
in this world of dreams,
this misty, moving dream of dreams?

For You

Where a hopeful, joyous thought
turns away from old pain
is where I feel you —
down deep
where your sure touch
unlocks the laughter inside my throat,
making me strike down the caution
in the air.
And I fling my secrets at your smiles
like a young girl
flapping her skirt in the sun.

Abraço

Times of spring madness
that rhyme with your eyes,
and full-bodied summer
when we love —
these I have
when my blood races
to hilltop holidays with you.
And I feel long before
you seek me in embrace,
I am there.
I am there.

Once

Warmly with me
in this afternoon's particular glow
of remembrance
you are here again
wordlessly telling me who you are
and I am listening, quick-breathed and close,
as we lean into easy understandings.

It was our time once.
We split the ripened melons
of the other's need
and set the table richly full
with what we thrilled to share.
There was no fear then, nor talk
of intervening worlds we knew would come
and finish us.

And now, though settled into separateness,
I can still have you here again, and mine,
as memory of you returns to me —
unseasonably and forever sweet.